A Tune A Day

FOR GUITAR.
BY C. PAUL HERFURTH.

BOOK ONE.

Exclusive Distributors:
Music Sales Limited
8/9 Frith Street, London W1V 5TZ, England.
Music Sales Pty Limited
120 Rothschild Avenue, Rosebery, NSW 2018, Australia.

Order No. BM10199
ISBN 0.7119.1570.9

BOSTON MUSIC COMPANY.

Contents

RUDIMENTS OF MUSIC

Music is represented on paper by a combination of characters and signs; it is necessary to learn all of these in order to play the Guitar intelligently.

Symbols called notes are written upon and between five lines  which is the staff.

The staff is divided by barlines into bars as follows. :

These, in turn, are equal in time value, according to the fractional numbers, (Time signature) placed at the beginning of the music. The different time signatures will be introduced throughout the book as the need arises.

The Treble or G clef  found at the beginning of the staff encircles the second line which establishes the note

G on this line, from which the other lines and spaces are named as follows:

In addition notes are written upon and between short lines above and below the staff. These lines are called leger lines.

A rest indicates a pause, or silence for the value of the note after which it is named, such as

Semibreve rest   Minim rests   Crotchet rests   Quaver rests

The end of a piece is indicated by a light and heavy line.

When a section or part of a piece is to be repeated it will be shown by a double bar with two dots.

Key Signatures, Sharps, Flats, and Naturals will be taken up and explained as the need arises.

HOLDING THE GUITAR IN PLAYING POSITION

IN SITTING POSITION

Sit erect in a straight chair and cross the left leg over the right knee. Place the guitar (lower curved part) on the left leg about halfway between the knee and the hip. Raise the neck of the instrument so that the head is approximately in line with your left shoulder. Hold the guitar rather firmly (but not tight) against the body with the right arm just below the elbow. The right hand and wrist should be completely relaxed.

Many performers prefer to cross the right leg over the left knee. Try both ways and use the one which is most comfortable for you.

THE LEFT HAND

THE LEFT HAND

Place the thumb against the under side of the neck approximately in line with the first fret. The wrist should be well arched bringing the hand above the strings. Allow the tips of the fingers to fall straight down upon the strings. THE PALM OF THE HAND SHOULD *NOT* TOUCH THE NECK.

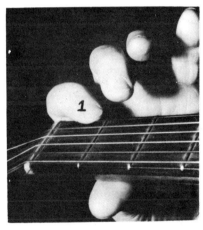

HOLDING THE PICK

HOLDING THE PICK

The pick (large rounded end) is held lightly between the thumb and curved first finger of the right hand. Use as little of the point as possible for the best tone. The more point you use the greater will be the string resistance thus resulting in a poor hard tone. Rest the little finger on the instrument to help support the hand. The strings are plucked with the pick slanting downward.

IN THE BEGINNING YOU MIGHT FIND IT EASIER TO PLUCK THE STRINGS WITH THE THUMB OF THE RIGHT HAND.

After you are able to locate the different strings readily you might try using the pick.

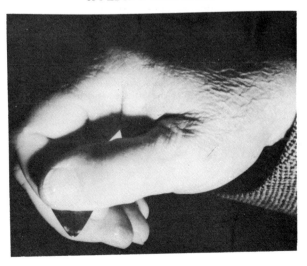

TUNING THE GUITAR

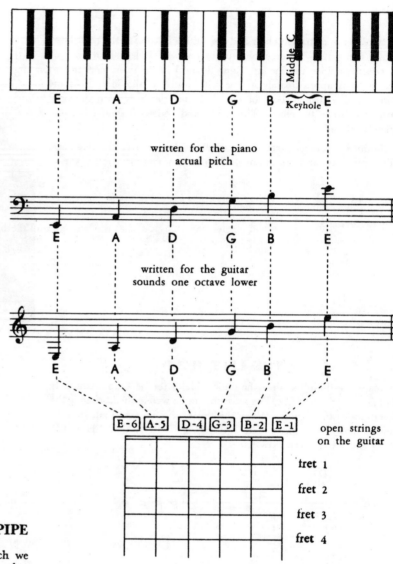

Piano keyboard

FROM THE PIANO

The six open strings of the guitar should be tuned to the same pitch as the notes shown on the piano keyboard. Note that middle (C) is just to the left of the keyhole.

written for the piano
actual pitch

written for the guitar
sounds one octave lower

THE ACTUAL PITCH OF THE GUITAR IS ONE OCTAVE LOWER THAN THE WRITTEN NOTES ON THE STAFF.

open strings
on the guitar

fret 1
fret 2
fret 3
fret 4

THE GUITAR PITCH PIPE

Pitch pipes giving the correct pitch of the six open strings are obtainable from music stores. WHEN TUNING FROM A PITCH PIPE BE SURE THE STRINGS ARE PITCHED ONE OCTAVE *LOWER* THAN THAT SOUNDING ON THE PIPE.

TUNING WITHOUT PIANO OR PITCH PIPE

As the lowest string (E) will vary the least in pitch we might use this string as a starting point and tune the other strings as follows (see Fig. 1):

Place finger just behind the 5th fret of the low (E) 6th string, and tune the 5th string to the same pitch. (A)

Stop the (A) string at the 5th fret and tune the 4th string to the same pitch. (D)

Stop the (D) string at the 5th fret and tune the 3rd string to the same pitch. (G)

Stop the (G) string at the FOURTH fret and tune the 2nd string to the same pitch. (B)

Stop the (B) string at the 5th fret and tune the 1st string to the same pitch. (E)

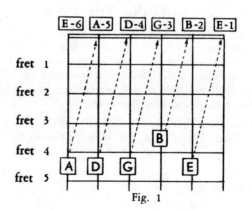

Fig. 1

THE SIX OPEN STRINGS OF THE GUITAR

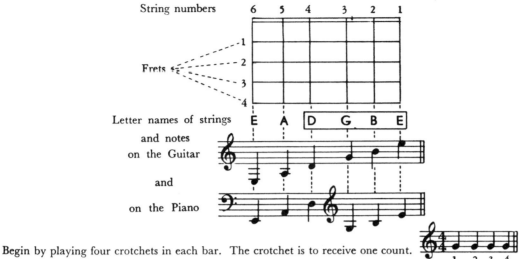

Begin by playing four crotchets in each bar. The crotchet is to receive one count.

The symbol for this method of counting is indicated at the beginning of the bar and called the time signature.

4 = ———— { Four counts in each bar.
time means
4 = ———— { Each crotchet receives one count.

STRIKE ALL NOTES WITH A DOWN (⊓) STROKE.

Start by using only the first four strings: (E 1st – B – G – D). | See diagram above. |

FOUR DOWN AND UP

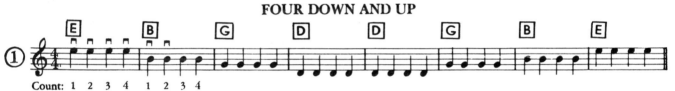

Count: 1 2 3 4   1 2 3 4

First recite letter names of notes as you play them, then repeat counting 1 – 2 – 3 – 4. Be sure to count evenly.

FOUR UP AND DOWN

Count: 1 2 3 4   1 2 3 4

TWO DOWN UP, DOWN AND UP

Count: 1 2 3 4   1 2 3 4

MERRILY

Using the open G & D strings.

Guitar

Count: 1 2 3 4   1 2 3 4

Piano

COUNTING THE BEATS: TWO-FOUR TIME

2 = _____ { Two counts in each bar.
time means
4 = _____ { Each crotchet receives one count.

REPEAT SIGN. Two dots :‖ before a double bar indicate a repeat to the beginning or to the last reversed repeat sign ‖: and play again.‖: Repeat   :‖

First recite letter names of notes while playing, then repeat, counting 1 – 2 evenly.

TWO DOWN TWO UP

ALL MIXED UP

TEN LITTLE IN'JUNS

AMERICAN SONG

JINGLE BELLS

PIERPONT

LIGHTLY ROW

NURSERY RHYME

THE FIRST STRING, E: FINGER-PLACING F (1st Finger) AND G, (3rd Finger)

HALF STEP E TO F, WHOLE STEP F TO G.

Place fingers firmly upon the strings just below (not on) the Fret (see illustration).

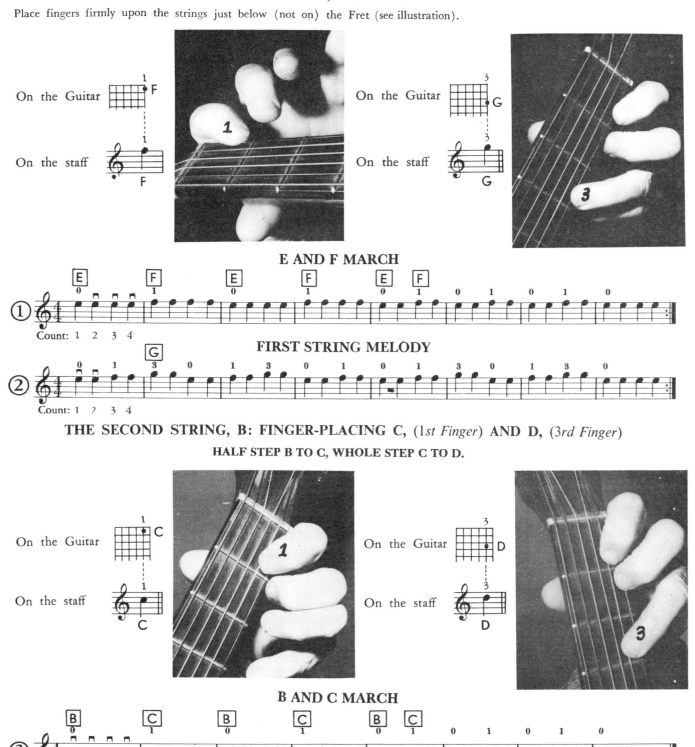

FAMILIAR MELODIES ON THE E, (*1st*) AND B, (*2nd*) STRINGS

A crotchet-rest (𝄽) receives one count, the same as a crotchet.
Recite the letter names of notes before playing.
* Hold fingers down until necessary to lift them.

OATS AND BEANS

OLD ENGLISH

FOLK SONG

FRENCH SONG

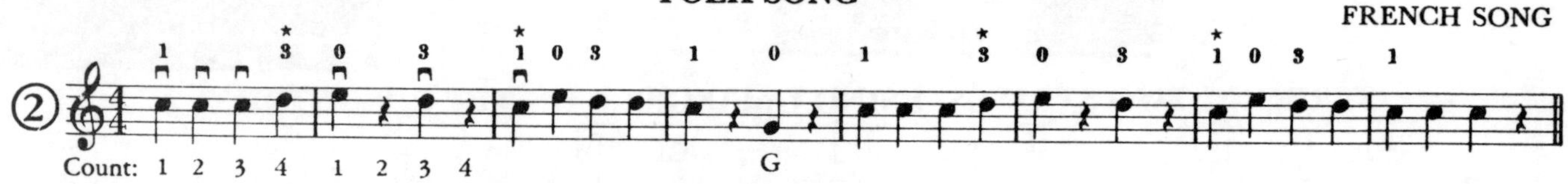

MERRILY

NURSERY RHYME

JINGLE BELLS

PIERPONT

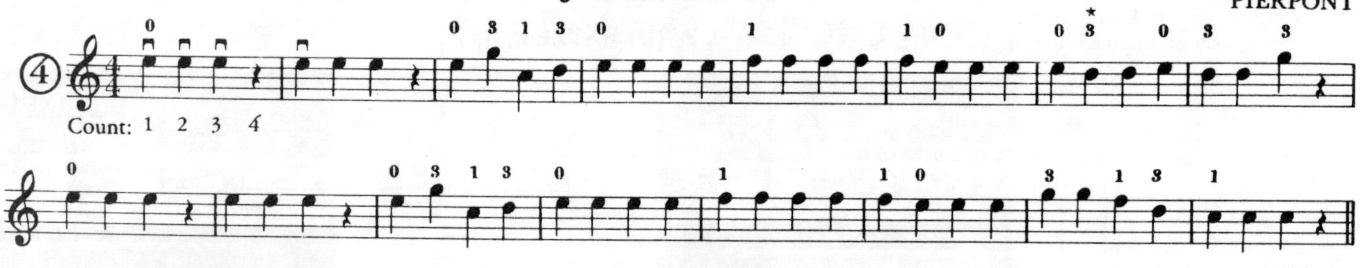

LIGHTLY ROW

FOLK SONG

SKIP TO MY LOU

AMERICAN SONG

THE DOWN (⊓) STROKE ON TWO OPEN STRINGS

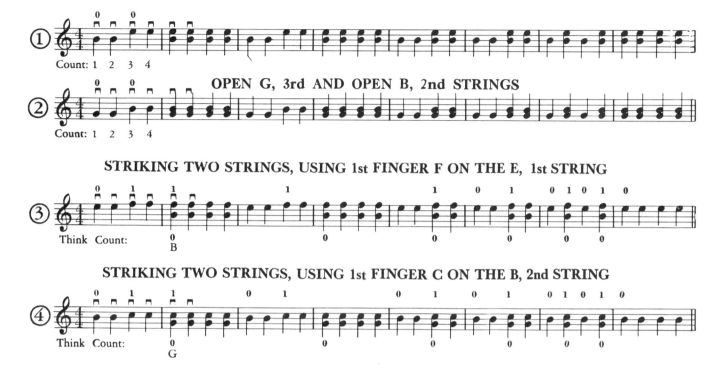

OPEN G, 3rd AND OPEN B, 2nd STRINGS

STRIKING TWO STRINGS, USING 1st FINGER F ON THE E, 1st STRING

STRIKING TWO STRINGS, USING 1st FINGER C ON THE B, 2nd STRING

STRIKING THREE-STRING CHORDS

When three or more notes sound together in harmony they produce a chord. It is most important that you learn and memorize the names as well as the fingering for each chord. STRUM ALL CHORDS WITH A DOWN (⊓) STROKE.

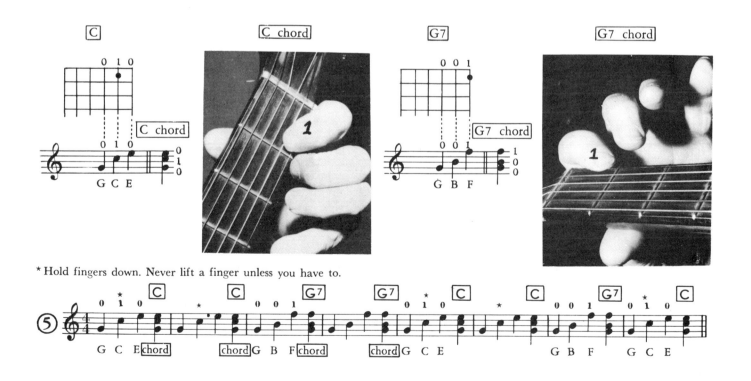

* Hold fingers down. Never lift a finger unless you have to.

SONG ACCOMPANIMENT
USING THE C AND G7 CHORDS

A CHORD MELODY

SONGS TO PLAY USING THE ABOVE TWO CHORDS

You are now ready to accompany many familiar songs and have fun playing the guitar. The songs on the following pages may be used as guitar duets or to accompany singing. PROCEDURE: (1) Play the melody line, (2) Play the chord line until you can play it without hesitating at a chord change, (3) Try to sing the melody line while strumming the chords. The melody line may be sung by a group, or played on any C instrument such as piano, violin, oboe or flute.

SKIP TO MY LOU

MOUNTAIN TUNE

SOME FOLKS DO

FOSTER

MORE SONGS TO PLAY USING THE C AND G7 CHORDS
MERRILY WE ROLL ALONG

8

THE THIRD STRING, G: FINGER-PLACING A (*2nd Finger*)
(Whole step G to A)

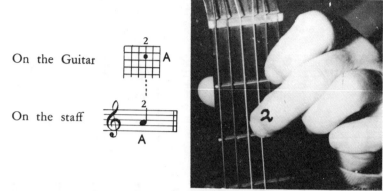

On the Guitar

On the staff

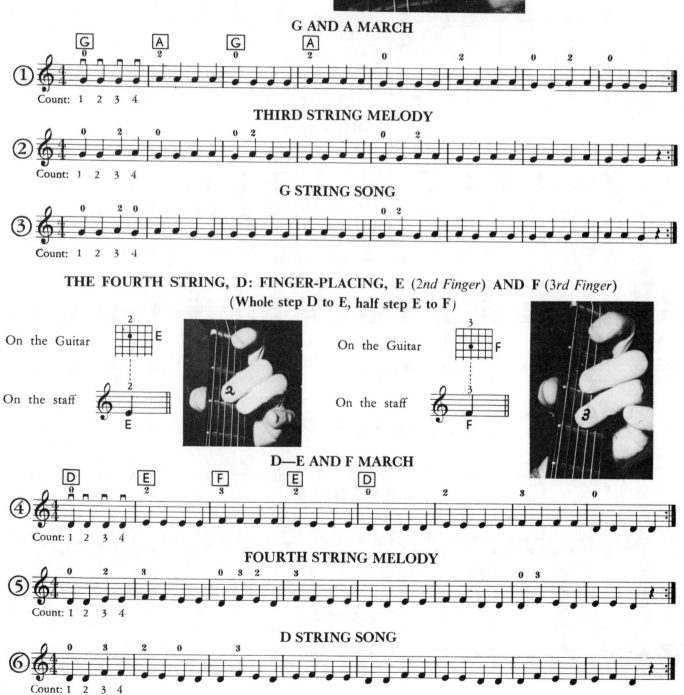

G AND A MARCH

① Count: 1 2 3 4

THIRD STRING MELODY

② Count: 1 2 3 4

G STRING SONG

③ Count: 1 2 3 4

THE FOURTH STRING, D: FINGER-PLACING, E (*2nd Finger*) AND F (*3rd Finger*)
(Whole step D to E, half step E to F)

On the Guitar

On the staff

On the Guitar

On the staff

D—E AND F MARCH

④ Count: 1 2 3 4

FOURTH STRING MELODY

⑤ Count: 1 2 3 4

D STRING SONG

⑥ Count: 1 2 3 4

MELODIES USING FINGERS ON THE D, (4th) AND G, (3rd) STRINGS

Learning the names and fingerings of the notes on this page will be most helpful in your later study of the guitar. Be sure to learn them.

THE KING'S CAROL

Count: 1 2 3 4 1 2 3 4

JUMPING JACK

Count: 1 2 3 4 1 2 3 4

IN THE MINOR

Count: 1 2 3 4 1 2 3 4

MORE OF THE MINOR

Count: 1 2 3 4 1 2 3 4

FINDING OUR WAY

Count: 1 2 3 4 1 2 3 4

AWAY WE GO

Count: 1 2 3 4 1 2 3 4

TESTING

Do you know your fingering?

Count: 1 2 3 4

THREE NEW CHORDS: G-D7 AND F

(Do you remember the C and G7 chords on page 5?)

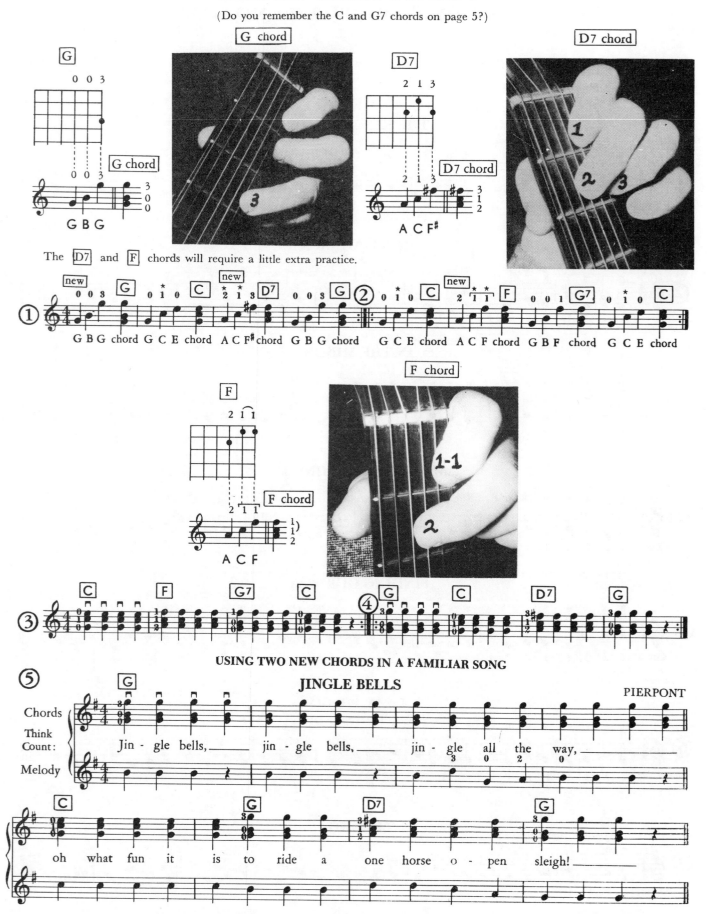

The D7 and F chords will require a little extra practice.

USING TWO NEW CHORDS IN A FAMILIAR SONG

JINGLE BELLS

PIERPONT

Chords
Think
Count:
Melody

Jin - gle bells,_____ jin - gle bells,_____ jin - gle all the way,_____

oh what fun it is to ride a one horse o - pen sleigh!_____

FUN WITH SONGS TO PLAY

CHORDS FOR THIS PAGE

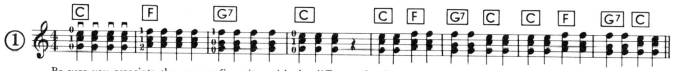

Be sure you associate the correct fingering with the different chord names.

Slanting lines  mean the chord is to be repeated on each beat of the bar until the next chord change is indicated.

BLUE-TAIL FLY

MINSTREL SONG

Jim Crack corn and I don't care, Jim Crack corn and I don't care,

Jim Crack corn and I don't care, old mas-sa's gone a-way, a-way.

LITTLE BROWN JUG

FOLK SONG

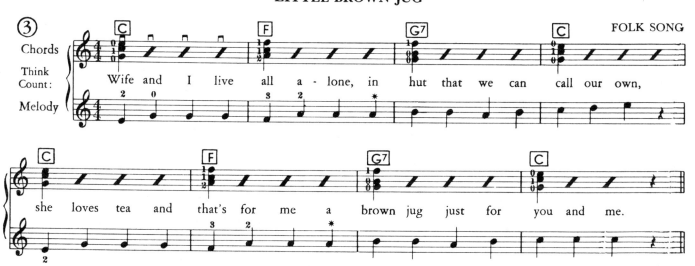

Wife and I live all a-lone, in hut that we can call our own,

she loves tea and that's for me a brown jug just for you and me.

MORE SONGS TO PLAY USING THE C—F AND G7 CHORDS

By this time you should know the fingering for these chords.

OLD MAC DONALD'S FARM

Music for Schools

A specially selected range of music books, tutors and reference books for schools and libraries. From folk to pop, jazz to classics, every book is graded according to age and ability.

The Complete Guitar Player
by Russ Shipton
For classroom or private use. Easy to follow text with diagrams and demonstration photographs. Special bands of colour focus the attention of the guitarist on the music. All songs or solos are on one page or facing pages. Most of the course is based on the music of modern performers such as Bob Dylan, John Denver and The Beatles. Enables you to play right from lesson one to an advanced stage, and assumes you have no knowledge of music.
Book 1, also contains pull-out chord chart and unique tuning record. *(CD), AM 25123*
Book 2 *(CD), AM 25131*
Book 3 *(CD), AM 25149*
Book 4 *(CD), AM 25156*
Complete set of separate books also available. *AM 25164*

The Complete Guitar Player
Omnibus Edition Books 1, 2, 3, and 4 *(CD), AM 26691*

The Complete Guitar Player Cassettes
Four cassettes in all, one to each book of The Complete Guitar Player.
Cassette: Book 1 *(CD), OM 20004*
Cassette: Book 2 *(CD), OM 20012*
Cassette: Book 3 *(CD), OM 20038*
Cassette: Book 4 *(CD), OM 20046*

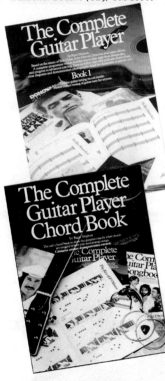

The Complete Guitar Player Chord Book
by Russ Shipton
Shows exactly what chords are needed to both play and arrange songs. Many clear photographs plus unique demonstration record.
(CD), AM 31717

Chord Book Cassette
This cassette supplements the contents of ''The Complete Guitar Player Chord Book''.
(CD), OM 20137

The Complete Guitar Player Video
Full colour teaching video lasting 60 minutes which is an important addition to The Complete Guitar Player series. A self-contained home study course.
VHS *(CD), OV 10002*
Beta *(CD), OV 10010*

The Complete Rock & Pop Guitar Player
Learn to play guitar in the style of Dire Straits, Duran Duran, Bruce Springsteen . . . right from lesson one. Easy-to-follow lessons, diagrams and demonstration photographs.
Book 1
Holding your guitar, tuning, chord changing. Pull out chord chart.
(CD), AM 60278
Book 2
Easy musical notation, tablature, rock and reggae strum patterns. Classic backing riffs, new chords.
(CD), AM 60286
Book 3
Introduction to harmony, new chords, arpeggio style accompaniment, modern rhythm styles, strumming effects.
(CD), AM 60294
Book 4
Electronic effects, new chords and backing styles, hammer-ons and pull-offs, new riffs, advanced techniques.
(CD), AM 60302

D.I.Y. Guitar Repair
by Pieter J. Fillet
Easy-to-follow instructions, plus 170 diagrams and photos. Slim format.
(CD), AM 38530

Guitar Case Chord Book
by Peter Pickow
Fits into your guitar case. Clear readable diagrams and no page flipping.
(CD), AM 35841

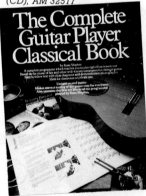

The Guitarist's Picture Chords
by Happy Traum
The most useful guitar chords in every key diagrammed in three different positions. The first position is accompanied by a photograph.
(CD), AM 16015

The Guitarist's Picture Chord Encyclopedia
by John Pearse
Every chord you'll ever need to play shown in photographs, diagrams and standard notation.
(CD), OP 41797

Instant Guitar: Play Today
Fastest way to learn guitar. Written in easy to follow language, it assumes no knowledge of music. Instructional record included.
(CD), AM 32517

The Complete Guitar Player Classical Book
by Russ Shipton
The complete method clearly explained in text and many demonstration photographs. A collection of tunes to play.
(CD), AM 38217

Solo Guitar Playing
by Frederick Noad
Instruction, including graded exercises, practice studies and a survey of the guitar repertoire etc.
(BD), OK 61994

Solo Guitar Playing Book 2
by Frederick Noad
Technique, sight-reading, musicianship for the intermediate guitarist. Plus graded exercises and practice studies and an advanced repertoire of thirty works.
(BD), OP 40591

Accompanying Tapes to Solo Guitar Playing
by Frederick Noad
Tape A: Exercises & Study Pieces, Page 43–Page 128.
(BD), OM20236.
Tape B: Exercises & Study Pieces, Page 130–Page 213.
(BD), OM20244
Double Cassette: Pack A & B.
(BD), OM20293

Tuning Your Guitar
by Donald Brosnac
Fits into your guitar case. Easy-to-follow text and diagrams – will do wonders even for the so-called 'tone deaf'.
(CD), AM 35858

Using Your Guitar
by Brook Hedick
Fits into your guitar case. Basic instruction, maintaining your guitar, tablature and song accompaniment etc. are some of the points covered in this comprehensive book.
(CD), AM 35783

Songbooks with Guitar & Piano Accompaniments

The Beatles Complete: Guitar
(I), *NO 17303*

The Beatles Complete (Revised)
Guitar/Vocal: Melody line chord boxes and symbols, 388pp.
(I), *NO 18145*

The Complete Guitar Player Songbook
Contains all the songs and music featured in The Complete Guitar Player. In standard notation with diagrams and chord symbols plus full lyrics.
(EI), *AM 26527*

The Complete Guitar Player Songbook No.2
This new book contains 50 songs which are arranged in keys which are examined in 'The Complete Guitar Player' books. Includes chords, left hand fingerings and right hand rhythm pattern, also lyrics.
(EI), *AM 31634*.

The Complete Guitar Player Songbook No.3
Another 50 songs by Paul McCartney, The Rolling Stones, Buddy Holly etc. In standard notation with chord boxes and full lyrics. Useful references to The Complete Guitar Player Course are printed with each song.
(EI), *AM 33291*

The Complete Guitar Player Songbook No.4
Of special interest to players who have followed The Complete Guitar Player Course. 50 songs by Billy Joel, John Denver, Elvis Presley etc. Standard notation, chord boxes and full lyrics.
(EI), *AM 33754*

The Complete Guitar Player Songbook No.5
Fifty songs by David Bowie, Bob Marley, The Police and many others in standard notation with chord boxes and full lyrics.
(EI), *AM 38027*

The Complete Guitar Player Songbook No.6
Songs from Elvis Costello, Sting, Mark Knopfler and other stars. Fifty numbers in standard notation with chord boxes and lyrics.
(EI), *AM 38209*

Animal Songs For Children
More than 40 animal songs beloved by children the world over. Melody lines in standard notation with chord names. New piano accompaniment.
(E), *AM 60062*

The Beatles Complete: Piano/Vocal, Easy Organ
Almost every song composed and performed by The Beatles. Plus original photographs and full colour illustrations.
(E), *NO 17162*

The Beatles Complete (Revised)
Re-engraved, revised edition of 'Beatles Complete'. 203 songs – composed and recorded by the group.
Piano/Organ: Piano/vocal, chord symbols *(E)*, *NO 18160*

The Joy Of Folk Songs
Contains eighty-two popular American songs and songs from other lands, all with lyrics and chord symbols.
(E), *YK 21061*

Nursery Rhymes And Songs
Over 40 nursery rhymes and songs. Illustrated throughout. Melody lines in standard notation together with chord names. Fun to learn and sing.
(E), *AM 60211*

It's Easy To Play Children's Songs
Seventeen songs for the modern child – to take their place alongside the traditional nursery rhymes. In easy piano arrangements with lyrics and chord symbols. Includes 'Banks of the Ohio', 'This Ole House' and 'Rivers of Babylon'.
(E), *AM 29489*

It's Easy To Play Christmas Songs
The world's best-loved carols and Christmas songs – twenty-one of them with words and chord symbols. Includes 'The First Nowell', 'Sleigh Ride' and 'Hark the Herald Angels Sing'.
(E), *AM 22641*

Hymns And Prayers For Children
Forty-two hymns and prayers. Complete with words, piano accompaniment and chord symbols. Easy to play.
(E), *AM 38639*

The Joy Of Disney
Easy piano arrangements of songs from Walt Disney's 'Bambi', 'Cinderella' and many others.
(E), *WD 10278*

Jumping, Laughing And Resting
Over ninety songs for children from 3-10 years old. Melody line in standard notation with chord names. Illustrated.
(E), *AM 38621*

The Lullaby Book
An illustrated collection of children's lullabies from all over the world. Easy-to-play arrangements with chord names and lyrics.
(A), *AM 37029*

New Songs For Children
Simplified arrangements of modern tunes such as 'A Windmill in Old Amsterdam', 'Grandad' and 'Yellow Submarine' – thirty in all. Words and chord symbols are included. Delightfully illustrated.
(E), *AM 13798*
Lyrics only *(E)*, *AM 30081*

New Songs For Children, The Gingerbread Man Book
Simplified arrangements of the kind of music today's youngsters like to sing and play. 31 songs arranged for piano/vocal with guitar boxes.
(E), *AM 36013*

The Nursery Rhyme Book
Over one hundred well-loved songs and rhymes. Easy piano arrangement plus words and chord symbols to sixty-four.
(E), *AM 26824*

Piano Collections & Keyboard Tutors

Classics To Moderns

Each of the six graded volumes in the *Classics to Moderns* Series presents a range of piano music exactly as written by master composers from early Baroque to the present day. The works are ideal for study, sight reading or simply for enjoyment.

Book 1 *(E)*, YK 20014
Book 2 *(E)*, YK 20022
Book 3 *(I)*, YK 20030
Book 4 *(I)*, YK 20048
Book 5 *(I)*, YK 20055
Book 6 *(I)*, YK 20063
Complete Set *(I)*, YK 20071

More Classics To Moderns

Easy, original piano music as written by many famous composers.

Book 1 *(E)*, YK 20121
Book 2 *(E)*, YK 20139
Book 3 *(I)*, YK 20147
Book 4 *(I)*, YK 20154
Book 5 *(I)*, YK 20162
Book 6 *(I)*, YK 20170
Complete Set *(I)*, YK 20188

The Complete Keyboard Player
by Kenneth Baker

Teach yourself to play any make of electronic keyboard, make your keyboard sound like a single instrument or a whole orchestra. Book 1 includes pullout keyboard chart and record.

Book 1 *(E)*, AM 38308
Book 2 *(E)*, AM 38316
Book 3 *(E)*, AM 38324

The Complete Keyboard Player: Songbook 1

Popular numbers to play on the electronic keyboard. Includes 'Brown Girl In The Ring', 'Cecilia', 'Eight Days A Week' and 'Mary's Boy Child'.
(E), AM 39116

The Complete Keyboard Player: Songbook 2

Nineteen popular melodies including 'Amapola', 'Every Breath You Take', 'Here Comes The Sun' and 'Top Of The World'.
(E), AM 39124

The Complete Keyboard Player: Songbook 3

Music for the electronic keyboard, with lyrics to 19 numbers such as 'Georgia On My Mind', 'Eleanor Rigby', 'Those Were The Days' and 'Thank You For The Music'.
(E), AM 39132

The Complete Piano Player
by Kenneth Baker

The only piano course based throughout on today's popular songs and famous light classics. Easy to follow text and clear demonstration diagrams. Book 1 with keyboard chart.

Book 1 *(E)*, AM 34828
Book 2 *(E)*, AM 34836
Book 3 *(E)*, AM 34844
Book 4 *(E)*, AM 34851
Book 5 *(E)*, AM 34869

The Complete Piano Player Collection

A unique collection of music. Each book is divided into solos, folk songs, etudes, sonatinas and duets.

Book 1 *(EI)*, PB 40831
Book 2 *(EI)*, PB 40849
Book 3 *(EI)*, PB 40856
Book 4 *(EI)*, PB 40864

Denes Agay's Learning To Play Piano

A progression of melodic pieces and studies teaching the basics step by step. This new course offers a fresh, unhurried, and sound approach to piano study as well as providing a melodic repertoire for the young player.
Book 1: Primer *(A)*, YK20845

Denes Agay's Learning To Play Piano
Book 2: *(A)*, YK20493

Denes Agay's Learning To Play Piano
Book 3 *(A)*, YK20501

Denes Agay's Learning To Play Piano
Book 4 *(A)*, YK20519

Start Playing Creative Keyboard
by Gabriel Butler and Mick Barker

Apply a few simple rules and techniques and discover a new world of creative playing on your keyboard. Useful tips and advice plus 16 famous popular songs.
(D), AM66663

Start Playing Keyboard
by Peter Lavender

An easy-to-follow course which starts you playing electronic keyboard right away, even if you have no knowledge of music. Includes 28 popular songs.
(E), AM 36906

Start Playing Keyboard Book 2
by Peter Lavender

Play 'fingered' chords with the left hand, improve your sight reading and playing technique and progress from SFX letter-note music to standard music notation. 16 popular numbers including 'We've Only Just Begun' and 'Yellow Submarine'.
(D), AM65749

Cats
The fabulous hit musical by Andrew Lloyd Webber. Based on 'Old Possum's Book of Practical Cats' by T.S. Eliot. All the songs arranged for piano with lyrics and chord symbols.
(BCD), AM 31006

Walt Disney Vocal Selections: Cinderella
Arranged for piano, with lyrics and chord symbols.
(B), WD 10039

The Jungle Book
Vocal selection arranged for piano/ vocal, with guitar chord symbols.
(ABC), WD 10013

Evita
Musical excerpts and libretto.
(CD), EVM 10005

Fiddler On The Roof
Vocal selections from the show. 11 numbers including 'If I Were A Rich Man' and 'Sunrise, Sunset'.
(D), AM 39520

Jesus Christ Superstar
Musical excerpts and complete libretto.
(CD), LE 11110

The New Illustrated Disney Songbook
Seventy-three memorable Disney songs from such favourite films as 'Snow White and the Seven Dwarfs', 'Pinocchio', 'Cinderella', 'The Jungle Book' and many more. Arranged for piano/vocal with guitar boxes. Full colour illustrations.
(CD), OP44031

Walt Disney's Bambi Songbook
All the songs from the film. Arranged for piano/vocal with chord boxes. Colour illustrations.
(AB), CC11321

Smike
Libretto *(B), AV 51860*
Vocal Score *(B), AV 51878*

The Walt Disney Songbook
Walt Disney favourites from 'Davy Crockett', 'The Jungle Book', 'Bedknobs And Broomsticks', 'Cinderella', 'Mary Poppins', 'The Happiest Millionaire', 'Pinocchio', 'Snow White' and other shows. 25 numbers for piano with lyrics and chord symbols.
(C), AM19316

The Complete Guitar Player Music Writing Book
The only music writing book specially compiled for guitarists. Enables you to keep a complete record of your own songs and repertoire.
64pp, AM 34208

The Complete Guitar Player Music Writing Pad
Sixty-four pages, each containing ten blank chord diagrams and 6 staves for notation.
64pp, AM 34216

Woodstock Music Manuscript Paper
A4, 12 stave, *32pp, WO 10166*
A4, 12 stave, spiral, *32pp, WO 10174*
A5L, 6 stave, spiral *32pp, WO 10224*
A5L, 6 stave stitched, *32pp, WO 10216*
A4, 12 stave, punched, *48pp, WO 10182*
A4, 12 stave, *64pp, WO 10190*
A4, 12 stave, spiral, *64pp, WO 10208*

The Complete Guitar Player Video
with Russ Shipton
Full colour teaching video lasting 60 minutes which is an important addition to The Complete Guitar Player series. A self-contained home study course.
VHS *(CD),* OV 10002
Beta *(CD),* OV 10010

How To Read Music
with Frederick Noad
Even if you have never read a note of music, this 51-minute, full-colour video will teach you how. Ideal for classroom or private teaching.
VHS *(CD),* OV 10028
Beta *(CD),* OV 10093

Jigsaw
Popular tunes for school orchestras. This series of flexible arrangements may be used with players of wide ranging abilities. Pack includes Conductor Score and parts for instruments including piano, recorder, violin, euphonium, cello, flute, bass, oboe and trumpet etc.
EastEnders (BC) AM65798
I Know Him So Well (BC) AM66747

We Wish You A Merry Christmas
by Barrie Carson Turner
Five variations scored for classroom ensemble and piano. This pack includes: piano/conductor score, 6 recorder and 4 each tuned and untuned percussion parts.
(BC) AM65202

Clarinet | Flute | Penny Whistle

Clarinet

Beatles, Themes And Variations: Clarinet
Seven Beatles themes with three variations. Pull-out piano accompaniment. Also for flute and trumpet.
(I), NO 17873

Graded Solos For Clarinet
Forty popular songs selected and arranged by Robin de Smet. Also for flute and trumpet.
(EI), AM 33598

Lennon & McCartney For Clarinet
This book presents over fifty compositions arranged for the clarinet. Also for trumpet and flute.
(I), NO 17725

100 Solos: Clarinet
Graded solos for players of all standards. Each piece is complete in itself and requires no piano accompaniment. Also for flute, saxophone, trumpet and violin.
(EI), AM 33689

101 Popular Songs For Trumpet And Clarinet
Arranged in solo and duet form. A collection of popular and traditional tunes.
(EI), HS 10445

The Complete Clarinet Player
by Paul Harvey
Based on popular songs and light classics. Clear text, diagrams, photographs.
Book 1
Blow your first notes and learn the rudiments of music. Play songs such as 'Love Me Tender', 'Yellow Submarine' . . . Fingering chart.
(CD), AM62613
Book 2 (CD), AM62621
Book 3 (CD), AM62639
Book 4 (CD), AM62647

Associated Board Examination Grades
(E) Elementary – Grades 1-3
(I) Intermediate – Grades 4-6
(Ad) Advanced – Grades 6-8
(T) Teacher's Book

Flute

Beatles, Themes And Variations: Flute
Seven Beatles themes with three variations. Pull-out piano accompaniment. Also for clarinet and trumpet.
(I), NO 17865

50 Selected Children's Classics
Includes 'Arabesque', 'Barcarolle' and 'Canon in D'. Also for recorder and piano.
(E), HS 10551

Flute Solos (EFS 38)
Effective arrangements of over 50 pieces. The wide range of compositions includes works of Beethoven, Brahms, Dvořák, Schubert and many others as well as folk songs, dances' jigs and reels from all over the world. Each piece includes piano accompaniment.
(BCD), AM 40197

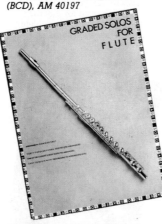

Graded Solos For Flute
Forty popular songs selected and arranged by Robin de Smet. Also for clarinet and trumpet.
(BD), AM 33812

Lennon & McCartney For Flute
This book presents over fifty compositions arranged for the flute. Also for trumpet and clarinet.
(I), NO 17717

100 Solos: Flute
Graded solos for players of all standards. Each piece is complete and does not require piano accompaniment. Also for clarinet, saxophone, trumpet and violin.
(EI), AM 33812

One Hundred And One Solos For The Flute
An outstanding collection of popular and light classical music arranged by Robin De Smet. Includes 'Chanson Triste', 'EastEnders' and 'The Power Of Love'.
(CD), AM63538

Selected Flute Solos (EFS 101)
This volume contains a group of the finest standard flute solos selected for their diversity in style and suitability for concert and contest use. Among the selections are works by Pessard, Chaminade, Mozart, Handel, Gluck, Fauré and Godard. All have piano accompaniment.
(Ad), AM 40403

The Complete Flute Player
by John Sands
The only flute course using popular tunes. Clear text, photographs and diagrams.
Book 1
Assembling the flute and producing your first sounds. Left hand notes, music notation and 7 keys. Music by Lennon & McCartney and John Denver etc.
(CD), AM62852
Book 2 (CD), AM62860
Book 3 (CD), AM62878
Book 4 (CD), AM62886

Penny Whistle

How To Play The Penny Whistle
by Gina Landor & Phil Cleaver
No previous knowledge required. Illustrated with clear diagrams. Also contains many popular tunes to play.
(E), AM 27137

The Penny Whistle Book
by Robin Williamson
A complete guide to the penny whistle for beginning to advanced players using a new systematic approach to fingering. Contains information on modal playing and 56 penny whistle tunes. Superb as a beginner's text, also of great use to the advanced player.
(EIAd), OK 63271

Recorder

Abba Songs For The Recorder
A selection of favourite Abba songs specially arranged for the recorder. Published complete with lyrics and guitar diagrams plus a two-page introduction to playing the recorder. Includes 'Waterloo' and 'Knowing Me, Knowing You'.
(I), AM 19720

Appalachian Folk Songs For Recorder
by Ralph Wm. Zeitlin
Thirty traditional folk songs and tunes arranged as solos and duets for soprano and alto recorders.
(I), AM 35650

Around The World With My Recorder
by Harry Dexter
Includes 101 selected song favourites in easy to play recorder arrangements.
(E), HS 11542

Bach For Recorder
by Cliff Tobey
Solos and duets arranged for soprano and tenor recorders.
(IAd), AY 15406

Baroque & Folk Tunes For The Recorder
An unusual collection of music arranged for the recorder – fifty pieces from over 300 years of music.
(I), AM 17948

Beatles For Recorder
Easy new arrangements by Robin de Smet, of famous Beatles songs. Thirty tunes with chord symbols.
(E), AM 18434

Beatles Songs For The Recorder
Outstanding collection of Beatles songs arranged specially for recorder. Complete with lyrics and guitar diagrams. Includes a two-page introduction to playing the recorder.
(I), NO 17394

Children's Songs For The Recorder
Twenty-five songs especially arranged for recorder with lyrics and guitar chord boxes.
(I), AM 13673

Christmas Songs For The Recorder
Over 20 of the best known Christmas carols arranged for recorder with lyrics and guitar boxes.
(E), AM 20157

Walt Disney Songs For The Recorder
Twenty-five outstanding selections from the shows and films which will always be associated with Walt Disney. Includes lyrics and guitar boxes.
(I), WD 10070

Early Music For Recorder
arranged by Robin de Smet
Easy new arrangements of airs and dances from the 10th to the 16th century. 47 tunes with chord symbols.
(E), AM 36542

Elizabethan Music For Recorder
by Ralph Wm. Zeitlin
Solos, duets, trios and rounds arranged for soprano, alto and tenor recorders.
(I), AY 15315

50 Selected Children's Classics
Includes 'Arabesque', 'Barcarolle', 'Canon in D'. Also for flute and piano.
(E), HS 10569

50 Songs For Recorder Book 1
For recorder with guitar accompaniment. Includes 'California Dreaming', 'Fernando' and 'Bright Eyes'.
(I), AM 29885

50 Songs For Recorder Book 2
For recorder and guitar accompaniment. Includes 'Top of the World', 'Little Buttercup' and 'Sailing'.
(I), AM 29893

Film Music For The Recorder
Twenty-eight well known film titles arranged for recorder, with lyrics and guitar boxes.
(I), AM 25701

Film And TV Themes For The Recorder
Over 20 notable tunes used as film and TV themes with lyrics and guitar chord boxes.
(I), AM 13962

Folk Songs For The Recorder
Twenty-seven famous folk songs arranged for recorder, with lyrics and guitar boxes.
(I), AM 29000

How To Play The Recorder
Pocket size recorder tutor which is a complete course for the beginner that is easy and fun to play.
(E), AM 35551

Hymns For Recorder
Easy new arrangements by Rôbin de Smet of 34 best loved hymn tunes. With chord symbols and words.
(E), AM 36559

Irish Music For Recorder
New easy arrangements by Robin de Smet of famous Irish songs and melodies. 30 tunes with chord symbols.
(E), AM 36534

Jazz For The Recorder
A contrasting selection of popular and jazz standards. Includes lyrics and guitar chord boxes.
(I), AM 28994

Paul McCartney: Songs for the Recorder
Twenty-seven songs including 'Mull of Kintyre', 'My Love'. With lyrics and guitar diagrams plus a 2-page introduction to playing the recorder.
(I), MY 70358

My Very First Recorder Songbook. Book A
Fifteen easy to play songs, folk tunes and songs from shows and films. With piano accompaniment and separate recorder part.
(E), AM 34158
Book B
(E), AM 34166

New Popular Songs For The Recorder
Published complete with lyrics and guitar chord boxes.
(E), AM 31501

Oliver: Songs For The Recorder
Outstanding selection from the show, with lyrics and guitar chord boxes, plus a six-page introduction to playing the recorder.
(I), AM 13368

Paul Simon Songs For The Recorder
Twenty songs including lyrics and guitar diagrams plus a two-page introduction to playing the recorder.
(I), PS 10016

Songs And Dances Of England
An outstanding collection of songs and dances from England's musical heritage. Arranged for voice and recorder, penny whistle or flute, or other suitable 'C' instruments.
(EI), AM 31428

Songs And Dances Of Ireland
A collection of songs from Ireland's rich musical heritage. All arranged for voice and recorder, penny whistle or flute, or other suitable 'C' instrument.
(EI), AM 31402

Songs And Dances Of Scotland
An exciting collection of songs and dances all arranged for voice and recorder, flute, penny whistle or other 'C' instrument. With chord symbols and guitar diagrams, plus full lyrics.
(EI), AM 31410

Cat Stevens Songs For The Recorder
Complete with lyrics and guitar boxes. Plus a two page introduction to playing the recorder.
(I), AM 23425

10 Famous Pop Songs For Recorder
For solos or ensemble playing. Piano accompaniment available. Can be played with any other instrument in the series. Includes 'Michelle' and 'Unforgettable'. Lyrics and chord symbols. Also for violin, saxophone, flute, clarinet and trumpet.
(E), AM 28614
Piano Accompaniments
(E), AM 28507

Together For Two Recorders And Guitar
A variety of music ranging from Purcell to Pop. Mozart's 'Allegro' is joined by melodies such as 'Clementine' and 'Rivers Of . Babylon'. With lyrics, chord symbols and guitar boxes.
Book 1 (E), AM 29901

Together For Two Recorders And Guitar
For C Recorders and guitars playing in ensemble. Boccherini's 'Minuet' to 'Yesterday'. Lyrics, chord symbols, and guitar boxes.
Book 2 (E), AM 29919

Associated Board Examination Grades
(E) Elementary – Grades 1-3
(I) Intermediate – Grades 4-6
(Ad) Advanced – Grades 6-8
(T) Teacher's Book

Continued . . .

Saxophone | Trumpet | Violin | Christmas Solos

Saxophone

101 Easy Sax Solos & Duets
A collection of popular and traditional tunes.
(E), HS 11864

100 Solos: Saxophone
Graded solos for players of all standards. Each piece is complete in itself and requires no piano accompaniment. Also for clarinet, flute, recorder, trumpet and violin.
(EI), AM 33697

The Complete Saxophone Player
by Raphael Ravenscroft
This course is based on popular tunes and light classics. With clear text, diagrams and photographs it will prove easy to understand even to those with no knowledge of music.
Book 1 (CD), AM62712
Book 2 (CD), AM62720
Book 3 (CD), AM62738
Book 4 (CD), AM62746

Trumpet

The Complete Trumpet Player
by Don Bateman
Based on popular songs and light classics. Clear text, diagrams, photographs.
Book 1
Rudiments of music, technique, the notes Low G to High D. Play songs such as 'I'd Like To Teach The World To Sing' and 'Edelweiss'.
(CD), AM39207
Book 2 (CD), AM39215
Book 3 (CD), AM39223
Book 4 (CD), AM39231

101 Solos For The Trumpet
arranged by Robin De Smet
An outstanding collection of music for trumpet covering a wide range of popular and light classical music.
(CD), AM61870

Popular Solos For The Trumpet
Over 30 hits from today's top artists. Includes 'Caribbean Queen', 'Walk Of Life', 'We Don't Need Another Hero' and 'When The Going Gets Tough'. No piano accompaniment required.
(CD), AM63108

Violin

100 Solos For Violin
Graded solos for players of all standards. The pieces are complete in themselves and require no piano accompaniment. Includes 'Dancing Queen', 'Michelle' and 'English Country Garden'.
(CD), AM33671

100 Cello Solos
Graded solos for players of all standards. The pieces are complete in themselves and require no accompaniment.
(CD), AM63231

Cello Solos
Easy to intermediate arrangements designed to bring out the finest qualities of the cello.
(CD), AM64486

Christmas Solos

Christmas Solos For The Clarinet
arranged by Robin De Smet
A unique collection of 49 traditional and up-to-date Christmas songs including 'Santa Claus Is Comin' To Town', 'When Santa Got Stuck Up The Chimney', 'Winter Wonderland' and many more. With chord symbols.
(CD), AM65020

Christmas Solos For The Flute
arranged by Robin De Smet
A unique collection of 53 traditional and up-to-date Christmas songs including 'Frosty The Snowman', 'I Believe In Father Christmas', 'Santa Claus Is Comin' To Town'. With chord symbols.
(CD), AM65038

Christmas Solos For The Recorder
arranged by Robin De Smet
A unique collection of 50 traditional and up-to-date Christmas songs including 'Away In A Manger', 'Silent Night', 'Santa Claus Is Comin' To Town' and 'Winter Wonderland'.
(CD), AM65046

Christmas Solos For The Bb Saxophone
arranged by Robin De Smet
A unique collection of more than 50 traditional and up-to-date Christmas songs including 'The First Nowell', 'Santa Claus Is Comin' To Town', 'Silent Night' and 'Winter Wonderland'. With chord symbols.
(CD), AM65061

Christmas Solos For The Trumpet
arranged by Robin De Smet
A unique collection of 49 traditional and up-to-date Christmas songs including 'Santa Claus Is Comin' To Town', 'When Santa Got Stuck Up The Chimney', 'Winter Wonderland' and many more. With chord symbols.
(CD), AM65053

Christmas Solos For The Violin
Standard carols and songs for the festive season arranged for the beginning-to-intermediate player. Chord symbols facilitate optional piano or guitar accompaniment.
(CD), AM67133

All books in this catalogue are available from your local music dealer.
In case of difficulty contact:
Music Sales Limited
Newmarket Road, Bury St Edmunds IP33 3YB.

MORE FUN WITH SONGS TO PLAY

"Pick up notes" or the Up Beat lead in. Notes at the beginning of a song before the first full bar are called "Pick up notes". The last bar of a song completes the time value of the first incomplete bar. Observe the count carefully. Review fingering of notes on the D and G strings on page 8.

COMIN' 'ROUND THE MOUNTAIN

Before playing "Buffalo Gals", be sure to review the G and D7 chords on page 10.

BUFFALO GALS

MORE SONGS USING THE G AND D7 CHORDS

(Refer to page 10 for diagrams)

BILLY BOY

NOTE VALUES: *SEMIBREVES AND MINIMS*

In order to play a melody in correct time it is necessary to sustain some notes longer than others. Up to this lesson you have been playing crotchets (♩) which receive one count. We now learn that MINIMS receive two counts and a SEMIBREVE receives four counts.

MINIM RESTS TWO COUNTS EACH   SEMIBREVE REST FOUR COUNTS

$\mathbf{C} = \dfrac{4}{4}$ = counts in each bar.
= each crotchet receives one count.

MINIMS—TWO COUNTS EACH

MINIMS AND SEMIBREVES

COMBINING THE NOTE VALUES ALREADY LEARNED
UP AND DOWN

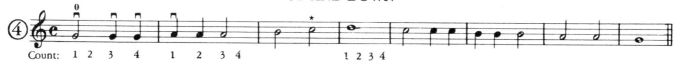

UNCLE NED

UP THE STAIRS

MELODY

CHANGING THE PITCH OF NOTES: SHARPS AND FLATS

SHARPS, FLATS,   A Sharp (♯) RAISES the pitch of the note to which it applies by a semitone or one fret.
AND NATURALS. A Flat (♭) LOWERS the pitch of a note by a semitone or one fret.
                         A Natural (♮) restores the note to its original pitch.

LEARNING TO USE F ♯ (sharp)

Remember that each fret on the guitar denotes one semitone or one step. To play a whole tone or whole step you must SKIP one fret. To sharpen a note use the next higher fret.

PLAY THESE TUNES USING F♯

Recite letter names of notes before playing.

LITTLE BROWN JUG

GOOD KING WENCESLAS

GOOD NIGHT LADIES

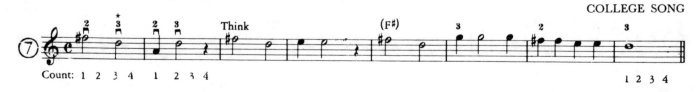

THE MAJOR SCALE

A musical scale is a succession of notes from a given note to its octave, eight notes higher. The form or progression of all major scales is as follows: Two whole tones, one semitone, three whole tones, one semitone. The semitones come between the 3rd & 4th and the 7th & 8th notes. The NATURAL half steps come between E & F and B & C (see scale below).

THE NATURAL OR C MAJOR SCALE
(not to be played at this time)

KEY SIGNATURES

Sharps (♯) or flats (♭) at the beginning of each line relate to the key signature. These sharps or flats affect all the notes of the same name throughout the piece.

ACCIDENTALS

A sharp or flat which does not belong to the key signature is called an accidental. An accidental applies ONLY to the bar in which it is placed.

LEARNING THE KEY OF G MAJOR (One sharp, F♯)

G MAJOR SCALE

FRENCH FOLK SONG

Hold 3rd finger down throughout

LIGHTLY ROW

Think F sharps and stretch your 4th finger.

ADDING THE OPEN D (*4th*) STRING TO THE G AND D7 CHORDS

For review of these chords see diagrams on page 10. Strum all four strings with a down stroke.

SONGS TO PLAY USING ABOVE CHORDS

RIG-A-JIG

OLD AMERICAN JIG

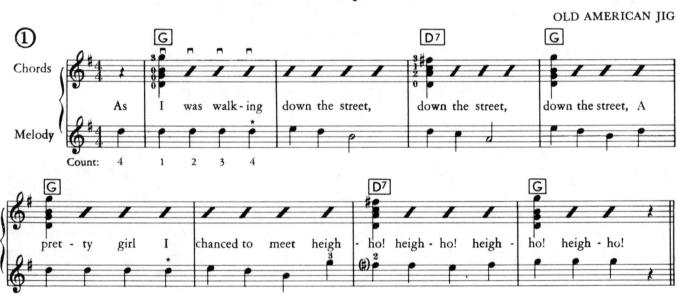

SHOO-FLY, DON'T BOTHER ME

CAMPBELL

A NEW RHYTHM: ¾ TIME

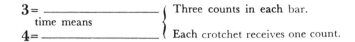

3 = ——————————— { Three counts in each bar.
time means
4 = ——————————— { Each crotchet receives one count.

A DOTTED MINIM (♩·) is equal to three crotchets and makes a full bar in ¾ time.

A TIE ⌢ or ⌣ when connecting two notes of the same pitch or sound, combines the value of both notes into one continuous sound.

ANDANTE

WITH APOLOGIES TO HAYDN

LITTLE ANNIE ROONEY

NOLAN

SONGS TO PLAY IN $\frac{3}{4}$ TIME (using four string chords)

CLAPPING SONG

MEXICAN FOLK SONG

DOWN IN THE VALLEY

KENTUCKY MOUNTAIN SONG

REVIEW: C-F AND G7 CHORDS (See page 10)
SONGS TO PLAY
CIELITO LINDO

FERNANDEZ

THE MAN ON THE FLYING TRAPEZE

NOTE VALUES: *QUAVERS*

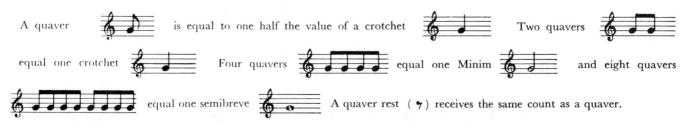

A quaver is equal to one half the value of a crotchet   Two quavers

equal one crotchet   Four quavers   equal one Minim   and eight quavers

equal one semibreve   A quaver rest (𝄾) receives the same count as a quaver.

Try using the down and up (v) stroke on repeated quavers of the same pitch when using the pick.

Observe carefully how to count quavers.

QUAVERS IN ⅔ TIME

Count: 1 + 2 +   1+ 2+

Count: 1 + 2 +   1 + 2 +

1 + 2 +   1 + 2 +

QUAVERS IN ⁴⁄₄ TIME

1 + 2 + 3 + 4 +   1 + 2 + 3 + 4 + 1   2   1 + 2 + 3 4

1   2 + 3   4 +   1 + 2 + 3   4

YANKEE DOODLE

AMERICAN TUNE

Chords   Yan - kee doo - dle   went to town   rid - ing on a   po - ny,

Melody

Stuck a fea - ther   in his hat and   called it mac - a - ro - ni.

SONG PRACTICE USING QUAVERS

D.S. AL FINE means to go back to the sign (𝄋) and play to fine (end).

LONG, LONG AGO

BAYLY

CAMPTOWN RACES

FOSTER

NOTE VALUES: *THE DOTTED-CROTCHET*

A DOTTED CROTCHET is equal in time value to three quavers ($\flat\cdot$ = $\flat\flat\flat$) Observe carefully the count for these notes as follows:

Play line A, compare it with line B, then play line B.

COMBINATIONS OF DIFFERENT RHYTHMS

IN 3/4 TIME

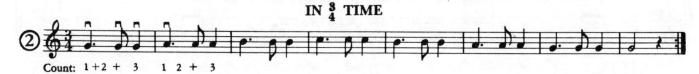

IN 4/4 TIME

IN 2/4 TIME

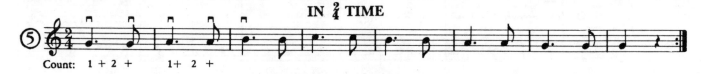

ALMA MATER

Always observe the key signature. It is a guide to the chords you will use.

COLLEGE SONG

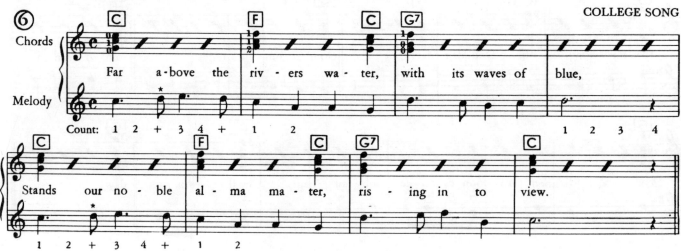

ADDING THE 4th STRING (D) TO THE C—F AND G7 CHORDS

Be careful in placing fingers that they do not touch the other strings.

FIRST AND SECOND TIME BARS. Play through to the repeat barring at the end of the 1st time bars. Return to the beginning and, after bar 6, proceed directly to the 2nd time bars.

DEAR EVELINA

COLLEGE SONG

MY DARLING CLEMENTINE

MONTROSE

26

SONGS TO PLAY USING CHORDS THUS FAR LEARNED

RED RIVER VALLEY

AMERICAN FOLK SONG

From this val - ley they say you are go - ing ___ We will miss your bright eyes and your smile ___ But re - mem - ber the red riv - er val - ley ___ And the girl that has loved you so true. ___

OLD FOLKS AT HOME

FOSTER

Way down up-on the swa-nee ri - ver, far, far a - way, Ther's where my heart is turn - ing ev - er, ther's where the old folks stay. All de world am sad and drear - y eve - ry where I roam, Oh! Dark-eys how my heart grows wea - ry, far from the old folks at home.

5th Fret

MORE FUN WITH MORE SONGS

Using a new chord A7 (study diagram).

HOME ON THE RANGE

COWBOY SONG

HAVE YOU MEMORIZED THE NAMES AND FINGERINGS FOR THE CHORDS ALREADY STUDIED? TEST YOURSELF ON THIS SONG.

BLOW THE MAN DOWN

SEA CHANTY

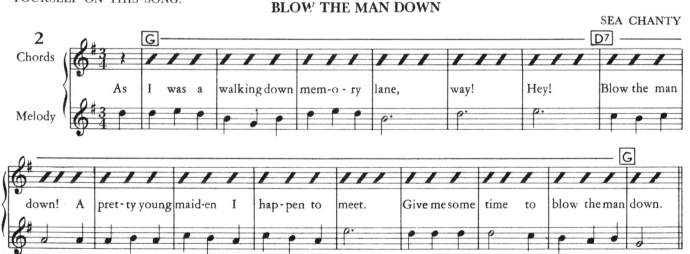

HOW WELL DO YOU KNOW YOUR FINGERING FOR THESE CHORDS?

OLD BLACK JOE

SILENT NIGHT

Printed in England by Commercial Colour Press, 7/89